Beyond the Blues

Prenatal & Postpartum Depression

A Treatment Manual

Shoshana S. Bennett, Ph.D.

Pec Indman, Ed.D., MFT

Moodswings Press

Published in the United States
Moodswings Press, 1050 Windsor Street, San Jose, CA 95129-2837
www.beyondtheblues.com

Contents

This book is dedicated to:

Henry
by Shoshana

He suffered with me through two postpartum depressions. He brought snacks to the children upstairs, so I could lead groups downstairs. He supported my career change, and parented Elana and Aaron as I helped that career grow. He typed my doctoral dissertation, cooks and cleans more often than I do, hangs up my clothes in the bedroom, and is a really nice guy.

Ken
by Pec

With my love and appreciation for your support and encouragement of my passions. When I've flown off to attend conferences or teach, work evenings, or had meetings on the weekends, you've held down the home front. You are my partner in work, home, and play.

Acknowledgements

We thank Jill Wilk, a postpartum depression survivor, who generously donated her time to this effort, as a labor of love. We also wish to thank Nely Coyukiat-Fu, M.D., and Jules Tanenbaum, M.D., for their review of the medical protocols. To our husbands, Henry and Ken, thank you for your technical support. To our children, Elana, Aaron, Megan and Emily, for teaching us about being moms. And to our dear clients, who trust us with their deepest fears and greatest hopes.

Shoshana S. Bennett, Ph.D.
510-889-6017
drshosh@attbi.com

Pec Indman, Ed.D., MFT
408-252-5552
pec@beyondtheblues.com

Preface

Postpartum depression (PPD), the most common perinatal mood disorder, is an illness that besets a significant number of women around the world. In the United States alone, over 3.5 million women give birth each year. Since the rate of PPD is between 15 and 20 percent, about 700,000 of these women will experience postpartum depression. The rate of gestational diabetes is between 1 and 3 percent and the rate of a Downs syndrome baby occurring in a 35-year-old mother is 3 percent. Curiously, we screen routinely for these conditions, which occur less often than postpartum depression, but we do not screen for postpartum depression, which afflicts up to one in five mothers.

While working in our communities, we have been asked numerous times to provide simple guidelines for assessment and treatment of perinatal mood disorders. Mothers and their partners have been seeking answers as to why a disorder is happening to them and what they can do about it. Many good books and journal articles have already been written on this topic. Our main goal is to summarize this information into a practical, easy-to-use format.

This manual is not meant to be used as a replacement for individual counseling, group support, or medical assessment, nor do we intend it to be a comprehensive textbook. While we feel this manual will provide critical information for psychotherapists and clients alike, it is not specifically intended to teach psychotherapy techniques for working with perinatal clients. That information deserves a manual unto itself, and will be created in the near future. We want, instead, to provide the most essential and up-to-date diagnostic and treatment information as concisely as possible.

ONE

Our Stories

We arrived at this professional focus by very different paths, one through personal suffering, the other through social activism.

Shoshana's Story

My husband Henry and I happily awaited the birth of our first child. We enjoyed a wonderful marriage and had planned carefully for the addition of children to our home. We had both grown up in healthy stable families with solid value systems. We were well-educated people with successful careers, my husband a human resources professional and I a special education teacher. I had worked with children for years, beginning with my first baby-sitting job at age ten. I felt quite confident taking care of children. The picture I had of my future always included children of my own. I prided myself on being a self-reliant person, able to manage well even under difficult circumstances. Henry came from a family of five children and had always planned on having a large family. We had many well thought-out plans for the future, and we looked forward with eager anticipation to being parents.

I felt terrific during pregnancy, both physically and emotionally. After childbirth classes, Henry and I felt prepared for the big event. There was one quick mention of C-sections and no mention at all about possible mood difficulties during pregnancy or after delivery. These classes were all about breathing techniques and what to pack in your hospital bag. On the top of every sheet on the note pad our teacher gave us appeared the words, "No drugs please." And it was also assumed, of course, that every woman would choose to breastfeed.

I endured five and a half days of prodromal labor (real labor, but unproductive), during which I could not sleep due to the discomfort. This was followed by another day of hard labor (still prodromal). My baby was transverse (sideways) and posterior ("sunny side up"), a position that caused severe back labor as well. I writhed as the sledgehammer-like pain hit to the front, then with no break, hit to the back. After not sleeping for almost a week, my insides were so sore and exhausted I thought I would literally die. Still not dilating, I was finally given a C-section.

My illusion of being in control was shattered. I had been a professional dancer, and my body had always done what I had wanted it to. The visual image I repeatedly had during this ghastly time was of a beautiful, perfect, clear glass ball violently exploding into millions of pieces. That was the self I felt I was losing. Hopelessness and helplessness replaced my previous feelings of control and independence.

I soon learned a skill that I would practice for years – acting. I bought into the myths that I was supposed to feel instant joy and fulfillment in my role as a mother, as well as an instantaneous emotional attachment to my baby. As my daughter, Elana, was placed in my arms, I managed to say all my lines correctly. "Hi, honey, I'm so happy you're finally here," I said, wanting to feel it (as I did later on). Inside, I was traumatized and numb.

Overwhelming feelings, fear, and doom intensified as my first OB appointment approached. While I drove to the doctor's office, my anxiety level rose to unimaginable heights. I pulled my car over to the shoulder of the freeway. Crouched over the steering wheel, I experienced my first panic attack. When I returned home and called to apologize for missing my appointment, I perceived only a tone of annoyance.

I had lost all the baby weight in the hospital, but just four months postpartum, I was forty pounds overweight. I had always enjoyed a wonderful working relationship with my OB, and felt that he respected me as an intelligent patient. Now, coming to his office as a hand-wringing, depressed mess, I felt embarrassed and vulnerable. As I sat in the waiting room surrounded by mothers-to-be and women cuddling their newborns, my feelings of guilt intensified. I became totally convinced that I should never have become a mother. Though my OB was well meaning, his technician-like manner was anything but reassuring. He focused primarily on my incision, not my huge weight gain or uncontrolled weepiness. With tremendous shame, I confessed some of my feelings to him, including, "If life's going to be like this, I don't want to be here anymore." I was shocked and hurt when he leaned back in his chair, laughed, and said, "This is normal. All moms feel these blues." He gave me his home number so I could call his wife, but he provided no referral. As my ten-minute appointment came to a close, I began to experience my first serious suicidal thoughts.

I did call his wife, who was convinced my problem was that the baby was manipulating me. I just needed to put her on a schedule. I also reluctantly joined a new-mom's group; since everyone was suggesting it, I decided to try. That was one of the most destructive actions I took. As I entered the room full of mothers cradling their babies with delight, I felt more alienated than ever. Discussing "problems" in this group meant pondering the best way to remove formula stains from fabrics, spit-up management, and calming a fussy baby. When I mentioned that I was having a bad time, an uncomfortable silence fell. I learned later that my name had been removed from the group's baby-sitting co-op. Upon leaving the first and only group session I attended, I felt more inadequate and scared than ever. Now I *knew* I was the worst mother that ever walked the planet.

Another complication was breastfeeding. Although my daughter latched on easily, I was overcome with pain due to inflammation and bleeding. I had been one of the "good" students who had prepared her nipples before birth, just as the nurses had suggested - rubbing them with a wash cloth to toughen them up. I asked a leader from a prominent lactation organization to help me. While the representative proved to be very helpful with suggestions about relieving the pains of breastfeeding, her emotional support immediately ended when I divulged that I would be going back to work in six months and would have to discontinue breastfeeding. She abruptly left my home. At this point I made the decision to stop breastfeeding completely, feeling like a total failure.

Life at home was frightening and unbearable. If I could sleep at all, I awoke in the morning in a full panic attack, wondering if I could survive another day. The simple act of watching television could turn an already dreary day into a deeper depression. The commercials portraying mothers in wavy white dresses, with naked babies in arms, taking delight in changing diapers and smiling angelically at their bundles of joy, sent me further into the depths. These were subtle reminders of the differences between all other mothers and me. When my husband left for work, I would beg, "Don't leave me, I can't do this by myself!" He would return from work to find me in the same emotional state as when he left. I still remember my husband peering in the front window each night with that worried look, trying to see how many of us were crying. If it was just one, it was me. Henry was frustrated with me. His mother, who had been a postpartum nurse for twenty years and who had popped out five babies of her own without the least dose of the "blues," was feeding Henry unhelpful information like, "Shoshana is a mother now. She needs to stop complaining and just do it." My respite came each evening as I tossed Henry the baby, proceeded to the driveway, jumped into the car, and sat and cried for a half-hour. There was no laughter, no humor, no friends, and no plans. There was only despair.

My mother had come to stay with us for the first three weeks.

She was wonderfully supportive but even with her therapist background, she did not recognize the signs of this serious illness. For the next year I continued on my downward spiral. I allowed no emotional or physical connection with my husband. I continued to be deprived of sleep due to insomnia and anxiety, ate without experiencing much taste, and just went through the motions with my daughter. I felt buried alive with no chance of clawing my way to the surface. I began seeing a psychologist, who never once requested any historical data on depression or anxiety in my family. All she did was probe for issues in my past, and if she couldn't find a real one, she would make one up. First she blamed my grandmother, then my sister. Finally she tried to convince me that having a Cesarean delivery caused my condition. I ended up feeling "crazier" than I did when I began. I swore I would never again open up to another professional.

When Elana was two and a half years old, my anxiety and depression began to lift significantly. "Maybe I *can* be a mother," I heard myself saying. My hair began to curl again for the first time since the birth. I began to enjoy my food and started seeing in color again, rather than shades of gray.

As with my first pregnancy, my second was flawless and without complication. I was enjoying my daughter by then, and the thought of a second child was a delight. After two days of prodromal labor, I decided on a C-section. The newfound enjoyment and relief from depression came to a crashing halt immediately after the birth of our son, Aaron. Although I could physically take care of him, my former "I'm incompetent" feelings returned. I would easily lose my temper at Elana, who was only three and a half years old. Having been a teacher and knowing child development, I could not find words for my shame and guilt at the way I was treating her. The brief amount of time she had her mom "all there" was suddenly ripped away from her.

In 1987, when Aaron was nearly six months old, Henry excitedly called me to look at a television documentary he was watching on postpartum depression. I was awestruck as the program described the disorder, its symptoms, causes, and possible cures. At the program's conclusion, I cried for an hour, looked at my husband, and said, "That's me!" The tremendous sensation of relief that someone had at long last described the turbulent agony I had been living felt like a weight being lifted from my whole body.

Equally important, I had finally heard that postpartum depression is diagnosable and treatable and that it can go away! If this condition is so common, I thought, where are all of us?

I started reading everything I could get my hands on, from all over the world, and realized that many countries were light-years ahead of the U.S. in recognizing and treating postpartum mood disorders. In my research, I came across Jane Honikman, founder of Postpartum Support International, in Santa Barbara. Jane generously offered me valuable information so that I could begin running a self-help group in the San Francisco Bay Area. Although I was still depressed myself, I was excited about what I had been learning and wanted to share my knowledge with other sufferers and survivors. In contrast to the new-mothers' group I had attended, my group would be a safe place for women to discuss their depression and anxiety openly, without fear of judgment. I posted two flyers, one at a local super market, the other at my pediatrician's office. The response was thunderous! Calls came in from all over Northern California, and some from as far away as Hawaii. Every week my living room was filled with six to fifteen women, desperate for support and guidance.

I became convinced that postpartum depression needed the same support, psychological attention, and medical tools as other mental illnesses. I made the decision to begin a new career devoted to the study and treatment of postpartum mood disorders.

For the past 14 years, the support groups, which commenced on my living room floor, have continued and flourished. As the current president of Postpartum Health Alliance, California's state organization, I am continuing to pursue my life's work.

Pec's Story

For as long as I can remember, I have been interested in political, emotional, and sociological issues as they relate to women. In the 1970s I trained as a family practice physician's assistant and worked in community-based family health clinics for a number of years. My interests varied, and my work took me to such places as women's clinics, an industry-based employee health center, a physical and fitness evaluation center, and weight management programs.

I entered a master's program in health psychology, and for the first time felt excited about school. I decided to continue and got a doctorate in counseling, getting my marriage and family therapy (MFT) license along the way. Many of my clients were referred by physicians, and much of my work with clients, particularly women, centered on issues related to health and emotional well-being.

One day, while in a physician's waiting room before a meeting, I came across a brochure from Postpartum Support International that described postpartum depression. I scribbled down the address, thinking, "I need to learn more about this." After receiving more information about PPD, I had a very mixed emotional response. I experienced sadness, extreme anger, frustration, and outrage. In all my years of training, I had learned nothing about perinatal mood disorders. I thought back to some of the women I had probably misdiagnosed. Why aren't health practitioners taught about PPD? My anger propelled me into action.

I have two daughters, and had a miscarriage in between. My second daughter was born when I was 40 after a work-up for infertility, a laparoscopy, and thanks to Clomid. My pregnancies went fairly well but both girls, each at 8.5 pounds, were delivered by C-section. The births were positive experiences. My older daughter was able to rock her new sister in a rocking chair in the recovery room as my husband, parents, and brother celebrated. I did have the "blues," yet they passed each time as my incision healed. I was fortunate to have a close friend on maternity leave at the same time, so we were together much of the time. All in all, my pregnancies, births, and postpartum experiences were positive. This only added to my outrage about PPD. All women should have the right to an emotionally and physically healthy pregnancy and postpartum experience!

My history of political activism served me well. I joined organizations and read books , attended conferences and trainings. Jane Honikman of Postpartum Support International told me about a woman in the East Bay, Shoshana Bennett, who was doing postpartum work. I called and asked if she would meet with me to make sure I was on the right track. She agreed, and we have been working together ever since.

This work has become my passion. I have never experienced so much personal and professional meaning and reward. I hope you will join us on this mission.

TWO

Pregnancy and Postpartum Psychiatric Illness

Perinatal (during pregnancy and postpartum) mood disorders are caused primarily by hormonal changes which then affect the neurotransmitters (brain chemicals). Life stressors, such as moving, illness, poor partner support, financial problems, and social isolation are certainly also important and will negatively affect the woman's mental state. Conversely, strong emotional, social, and physical support will greatly facilitate her recovery.

Any of the five postpartum mood disorders discussed in this chapter can also occur during pregnancy. These perinatal mood disorders behave quite differently from other mood disorders because the hormones are fluctuating. A woman with a perinatal mood disorder often feels as if she's "losing it," since she can never predict how she will feel at any given moment. For instance, at 8 A.M., she may be gripped with anxiety, at 10 A.M. feel almost normal, and at 10:30 A.M. become depressed and lethargic.

Our clients who have had personal histories of depression tell us that postpartum depression feels very different (and usually much worse) than depressions at other times in their lives. One of Shoshana's postpartum clients is a survivor of breast cancer. At a support group she beautifully explained:

When I had cancer, I thought that was the worst experience I could ever have. I was wrong — this is. With cancer, I allowed myself to ask for and receive help, and expected to be depressed. My friends and family rallied around me, bringing me meals, cleaning my house, and giving me lots of emotional support. Now, during postpartum depression, I feel guilty asking for help and ashamed of my depression. Everyone expects me to feel happy and doesn't accept that this illness is just as real as cancer.

Women who experience these symptoms need to speak up and be persistent in getting proper care. In the past, these illnesses have been trivialized and even dismissed. Research has shown how important it is to treat perinatal mood disorders for the health and well-being of the mother, baby, and entire family.

The Psychiatric Issues of Pregnancy

Contrary to popular mythology, pregnancy is not always a happy glowing experience! Approximately 10 percent of pregnant women experience depression. Of these, about 15 percent are so severely depressed that they attempt suicide.

It can be confusing that normal pregnancy experiences such as fatigue, appetite changes, and poor sleep are similar to symptoms of mood disorders. It is easy to make a blanket dismissal of these symptoms as just part of pregnancy. However, for that 10 percent, it is essential that the proper questions are asked and intervention is given when symptoms are outside the normal realm. When symptoms of depression or other mood disorders cause limitations in the client's ability to function on a day-to-day basis, intervention is necessary. This may include traditional (counseling and medication) or nontraditional modalities (such as Yoga or acupressure), or any combination thereof. The goal is to use whatever the individual woman needs in order to feel like herself again.

Depression during pregnancy has been associated with low birth weight (less than 2,500 grams) and preterm delivery (less than 37 weeks). Severe anxiety during pregnancy may cause harm to a growing fetus due to constriction of the placental blood vessels and higher cortisol levels.

Some women become pregnant while already taking psychotropic medications for depression, anxiety, and other mood problems. Many of these medications are considered acceptable during pregnancy. A practitioner who is familiar with the current research about the safety of taking medications during pregnancy should be consulted. Often it is safer to continue a medication than risk a relapse.

The rate of relapse for a major depressive disorder (MDD) in women who discontinue their medication before conception is between 50-75 percent. The rate of relapse for MDD in those who discontinue medications at conception or in early pregnancy is 75 percent, with up to 60 percent relapsing in the first trimester. In one study, 42 percent of women who discontinued medications at conception resumed medications at some time during their pregnancy. Resources listed in the back of this manual provide helpful guidelines regarding the use of medications.

Postpartum Psychiatric Illnesses

There are five postpartum mood disorders. The "blues" is not considered a disorder, since the majority of mothers experience it. This list details each of the principal disorders, some of their most common symptoms, and risk factors. It is important to note that symptoms and their severity can change over the course of an illness.

Postpartum "Blues"

- Occurs in about 80 percent of mothers
- Usual onset within first week postpartum
- Symptoms may persist from several days to up to six weeks

Symptoms
- Mood instability
- Weepiness
- Sadness
- Anxiety
- Lack of concentration
- Feelings of dependency

Etiology
- Rapid hormonal changes
- Physical and emotional stress of birthing
- Physical discomforts
- Emotional letdown after pregnancy and birth
- Awareness and anxiety about increased responsibility
- Fatigue and sleep deprivation
- Disappointments including the birth, spousal support, nursing, and the baby

Postpartum Depression and/or Anxiety

- Occurs in 15 to 20 percent of mothers
- Onset is usually gradual, but it can be rapid and occur any time in the first year

Symptoms
- Excessive worry or anxiety
- Irritability or short temper
- Feeling overwhelmed, difficulty making decisions
- Sad mood, feelings of guilt, phobias
- Hopelessness
- Sleep problems (often woman cannot sleep or sleeps too much), fatigue
- Physical symptoms or complaints in excess of, or without, physical cause
- Discomfort around the baby or a lack of feeling towards the baby
- Loss of focus and concentration (may miss appointments, for example)
- Loss of interest or pleasure, decreased libido
- Changes in appetite; significant weight loss or gain

Risk factors
- 50 to 80 percent risk if previous postpartum depression
- Depression or anxiety during pregnancy
- Personal or family history of depression
- Abrupt weaning

- Social isolation or poor support
- History of premenstrual syndrome (PMS) or premenstrual dysphoric disorder (PMDD)
- Mood changes while taking birth control pill or fertility medication, such as Clomid
- Thyroid dysfunction

Postpartum Obsessive-Compulsive Disorder (OCD)

- 3 to 5 percent of new mothers develop obsessive symptoms

Symptoms
- Intrusive, repetitive, and persistent thoughts or mental pictures
- Thoughts often are about hurting or killing the baby
- May include counting, checking, or other repetitive behaviors
- Tremendous sense of horror and disgust about these thoughts (ego-alien)
- Thoughts may be accompanied by behaviors to reduce the anxiety (for example, hiding knives)

Risk factors
- Personal or family history of OCD

Postpartum Panic Disorder

- Occurs in about 10 percent of postpartum women

Symptoms
- Episodes of extreme anxiety
- Shortness of breath, chest pain, sensations of choking or smothering, dizziness
- Hot or cold flashes, trembling, palpitations, numbness or tingling sensations
- Possible restlessness, agitation, or irritability
- During attack the woman may fear she is going crazy, dying, or losing control
- Panic attack may wake her up
- Often no identifiable trigger for panic
- Excessive worry or fears (may center around fear of more panic attacks)

Risk factors
- Previous history of anxiety or panic disorder
- Thyroid dysfunction

Postpartum Psychosis

- Occurs in one to three per thousand
- Onset usually about three days postpartum
- This disorder has a 5 percent suicide and 4 percent infanticide rate

Symptoms
- Visual or auditory hallucinations
- Delusional thinking (for example, about infant death, denial of birth, or need to kill baby)
- Delirium and/or mania

Risk factors
- Personal or family history of psychosis, bipolar disorder, or schizophrenia
- Previous postpartum psychotic or bipolar episode

Postpartum Posttraumatic Stress Disorder

- There is no available data regarding the prevalence or onset

Symptoms
- Recurrent nightmares
- Extreme anxiety
- Reliving past traumatic events (for example, sexual, physical, emotional, and childbirth)

Risk factors
- Past traumatic events

Perinatal Loss

No matter how a pregnancy is terminated, whether by nature or by choice, depression and anxiety commonly follow. Not only should grief be addressed through counseling, but medications may also be useful in reducing symptoms due to loss and hormonal changes.

When a stillbirth or neonatal death occurs, depression is, of course, to be expected. Counseling for the couple is essential, and medications should be considered to treat anxiety and depression. These women need to be monitored carefully for emotional symptoms in subsequent pregnancies and the postpartum period.

THREE

To the Women

In the chapters to follow, we will discuss the role of practitioners and partners in helping mothers recover. This chapter is for you, the sufferers.

Among the women we treat are those in the healthcare and educational professions, such as M.D.'s, nurses, daycare and preschool providers, teachers, and therapists, to name a few. We often hear from these women, "This can't be happening to me! I take care of everyone else in crisis." What we tell them is that our hormones don't care what we do for a living! No one is immune. No matter what the educational or socioeconomic level, culture, religion, or personality, wherever women are having babies, the statistics remain consistent.

Women who suffer postpartum emotional difficulty experience their anguish in many different ways. Here are some of the common feelings they express:

- "No one has ever felt as bad as I do."
- "I'm all alone. No one understands."
- "I'm a failure as a woman, mother, and wife."
- "I'll never be myself again."
- "I've made a terrible mistake."
- "I'm on an emotional roller coaster."
- "I'm losing it."

Please know that each woman may experience these feelings at varying levels. Some may feel all of them, and others may feel only a few. You might also recognize some of your symptoms listed in chapter 2.

Finding Help

We encourage you to contact Postpartum Support International (PSI) at (805) 967-7636 or www.postpartum.net to locate a therapist who has shown interest and commitment in the postpartum field. PSI provides specialized training in perinatal mood disorders. We have not found any graduate training that covers this material. Do not assume (as many insurance companies would like you to believe) that someone who has expertise in working with depression or other mood disorders is knowledgeable about perinatal mood disorders.

Sometimes an insurance company is willing to add a specialist to its provider list or pay for you to see one. If your insurance company will pay only if you see providers on their list, here are screening questions to help you determine their knowledge in this area. It's important to ask these questions, even if the therapist considers himself or herself knowledgeable. If you don't have the energy to deal with the insurance company or screening professionals, ask a support person to do this for you.

- What specific training have you received in postpartum mood disorders?
- Do you belong to any organization dedicated to education about perinatal mood disorders? (Someone committed to work in this field should belong to at least

one of these organizations: Postpartum Support International, Postpartum Health Alliance, Depression After Delivery, Marcé Society, North American Society for Psychosocial OB/GYN.)

- What books do you recommend to women with postpartum depression or anxiety? (Someone with expertise should be able to name several books listed in the Resources section of this manual.)
- What is your theoretical orientation? (Research has shown the most effective types of therapy for your condition are cognitive-behavioral and interpersonal. You are experiencing a life crisis; long-term intensive psychoanalysis is not appropriate.)

If you are unable to find a therapist with expertise, interview until you find someone you feel is compassionate and willing to learn. Be a good consumer. Shop around until you feel comfortable.

The Truth of the Matter

As you face the challenge of a postpartum mood disorder, remind yourself of these truths:

- *I will recover!* We have never met a woman who, after proper treatment, did not recover.
- *I am not alone!* One in five women will experience a postpartum reaction more severe than the "baby blues."
- *This is not my fault!* You did not create this; it is a biochemical illness.

- *I am a good mom!* The fact that you are trying to improve the quality of your life and your family's proves you are a good mom.
- *It is essential for me to take care of myself!* It is your job to take care of yourself so you can get better and take care of your family.
- *I am doing the best I can!* No matter what your current level of functioning, you are taking steps, regardless of how small they seem. Good for you!

Depression may interfere with your ability to believe these statements, so it is important to say them frequently, as if you really mean them. As you recover, this exercise will become easier.

Basic Mom Care

Finding Support People

Very often when we are in crisis, we overlook the people around us who can be of help and support. People can support you in different ways. Support may be physical; for instance, cooking, cleaning, caring for the baby, shopping, taking you for a walk or to an appointment. Emotional support may include sitting and listening, hugging, and giving encouraging words.

Even though the following writing task may feel overwhelming, it can serve to create your lifeline. This is a brainstorming exercise — write down everyone who comes to mind, regardless of the type of support they may be able to give you. If possible, do this exercise with a support person. Keep this list of supporters' names and phone numbers handy by your phone for times of need.

Here are some places where our clients have found people

for their support network:
- Partner
- Family and extended family
- Neighbors
- Co-workers
- Religious communities
- Professionals (including doulas, lactation consultants, nannies, housekeepers)
- Hotlines
- Internet chatrooms (Warning: If you are anxious or obsessive we do not recommend)
- Postpartum depression support groups

Eating

Often women with postpartum depression and anxiety crave sweets and carbohydrates. If you can eat something nutritious, especially protein, each time you feed the baby, you can help keep your blood sugar level even. This will contribute to keeping your mood stable. We understand this may be difficult if you are experiencing a lack of appetite, so do the best you can. If you have trouble eating, try drinking your food—for example, protein shakes or drinks, but nothing caffeinated. Ask a support person to stock your refrigerator with things like yogurt, sliced deli meats and cheese, hardboiled eggs, precut vegetables, and fruit. Better yet, if they are not already offering, ask people to bring you food. Don't forget to drink water—dehydration can increase anxiety. Appetite problems are quite common with postpartum depression and anxiety. Please tell your health practitioner about any appetite changes. It might be helpful to consult a nutritionist who is familiar with depression and anxiety when you have the energy.

Sleeping

Nighttime sleep is the most valuable sleep in helping you recover. Five hours of uninterrupted sleep per night is required for brain restoration because it gives you a full sleep cycle. You will need to enlist a support person to be responsible for the baby during this time. The baby can be fed with breast milk or formula in a bottle. Remember, it is your job to take care of yourself. Even if you cannot arrange for this nightly, a few nights a week will help. If you are able to nap in the day, do so, but it does not replace nighttime sleep. Sleep problems occur frequently with mood disorders. If you are unable to sleep at night when everyone else is sleeping, please talk to your health practitioner. Medication will be helpful.

Activity

Even a few minutes of brisk physical activity can help your mood. When you are physically able to be active, find something you are willing to do (for example, walking, dancing, or bike riding). Even if the thought of walking around the block is overwhelming, don't feel like a failure. It will get easier as you feel better. If you know you would feel better if you did the activity, but it is hard to mobilize yourself, designate a support person to encourage and participate with you.

Taking Breaks

The myth is that if we really love our children, we wouldn't need breaks from them. This isn't the case.

We've bought into the idea that taking time for ourselves is selfish and bad, and therefore we feel guilty when we even think we need a break. The truth is that all good mothers take breaks - that's how they stay good mothers! We strongly recommend that you get regularly scheduled time off at least three times a week for a minimum of two hours at a time. For every job other than being a mother, breaks are mandated by law, and you'd expect much more time off. If you don't recharge your batteries, you'll be running on empty. You are not the only one who can care for the baby. Partners and family members, for instance, should be given alone time to bond with the baby too. This experience is important for the baby, and it can be done more easily with you somewhere else. Everyone wins.

If you're too depressed or tired to actually leave the house, go to another room and use earplugs or earphones. Or, maybe your support person can leave the house with the baby and give you alone time.

Going Outside

When we're depressed or anxious, the four walls feel as if they're closing in. Our world feels darker and smaller. We tend to fold in emotionally and physically (as in crossing our arms, hunching over, and fixing our gaze downward).

To counter this, go outside your home, look up at the sky, stand up straight, put your arms at your sides, and breathe. You don't have to actually go anywhere. Just go outside once a day, even if this means standing outside your front door in your bathrobe.

Scripts

You may not know what you need when a support person asks, "What can I do?" It's all right to say, "I don't know what I need right now. I just know I feel awful." Don't assume anyone can read your mind. You are most likely to get what you need if you ask for it. Try giving your partner, family, and friends a script. Scripts can be helpful in teaching what to say and not say to best support you. For example, when you are experiencing anxiety, it will not be helpful to hear, "just calm down and relax." Instead, try giving them suggestions of what to say and do:

- "I am sorry you are suffering."
- "We will get through this."
- "I am here for you."
- Hug.
- "This will pass."

A script does not detract from the genuineness of caring and love. On the contrary, it will give your support people an effective way to give you what you need. People who love you want you to get better. They will be relieved to know what will help.

For Women with Anxiety or Obsessions

Be sure to avoid caffeine and keep your blood sugar level even (see section above on eating). For many women with anxiety or obsessions, information provides fuel for worry. Turn off the TV news, and don't read the news section of the newspaper. Don't read books, magazines, or Internet information about postpartum mood disorders if you find it makes you more anxious. If you go to the movies, select comedies. Find activities that can soothe or distract you, rather than those that stir up anxiety.

Taking Care of Your Baby

Myth: *"I can't be a good mom unless I nurse my baby."*

The truth is there is no one right way to feed your baby. Whatever works for you and your family is the right way. There is a tremendous amount of pressure on new moms in our society to nurse exclusively, regardless of physical or emotional obstacles. We believe that one size never fits all. Whether you feed your baby breast milk or formula has no relationship to how much you love your child or what kind of mother you are. There are advantages and disadvantages to both breastfeeding and bottlefeeding, and some combination of the two may work for you as well. For instance, having a support person bottlefeed with formula or breast milk so you can be off duty is a responsible choice for your family's well-being. Don't allow yourself to be guilt-tripped! Be prepared for intrusive and inappropriate questions and comments about how you're feeding your baby. This may happen anywhere, for example, out in public, at your health practitioner's office, a mom's group, or at a family gathering. If any person, whether lay or professional, seems judgmental about the plan you've chosen, remind yourself that you have made the best decision you can for you and your family. You can ignore the question or comment or change the subject. Alternatively, you can say, "It's none of your business," "I can't breastfeed. I have a life-threatening illness," "I chose not to," or "My doctor told me I can't."

Remember, you are entitled to respond any way you need in order to get inquisitors off your back. You have nothing to apologize about. Good moms make sure their babies are fed. Period.

Myth: *"My baby won't bond if I don't nurse."*
If this were true, there would be whole generations of adults who never bonded with their mothers! Some women actually begin to bond with their babies when they stop breastfeeding. For women who are experiencing anxiety or pain related to breastfeeding, bottlefeeding may allow this time together to be more relaxed and enjoyable. There are no rules about how to bottlefeed. If you desire skin-to-skin contact, you can bottle feed bare-chested.

Myth: *"My baby can sense my depression or anxiety."*
Your baby cannot read your mind! Your thoughts or feelings will not damage your baby or the relationship with your baby.

What babies can sense is temperature, hunger, wetness, and physical contact. Your baby will feel close to you regardless of depressed or anxious thoughts running through your head.

Myth: *"Bonding happens immediately at birth."*
If this were true, no adopted children would ever bond with their adoptive moms. There is no one magic moment of opportunity when bonding must happen, and no reason to worry about bonding if you were unable to touch or hold your baby immediately after delivery. Even if your depression or anxiety has made it difficult for you to care for your baby, it's never too late. Bonding is a process of familiarity, closeness, and comfort that continues for years.

FOUR

For the Partners

This chapter is designed to provide support to you, the partner, regardless of your gender or marital status. To avoid confusion, we sometimes refer to the new mother as "wife." The sooner you become involved in the recovery process, and the greater your involvement, the more you both will benefit - together and separately. The more you understand what she is experiencing, the better supported she will feel. That will, in turn, expedite her recovery.

Some Things to Keep in Mind

- *You didn't cause her illness and you can't take it away.* Postpartum depression and anxiety is a biochemical disorder. It is no one's fault. When her brain chemistry balances, she will feel like herself again. It is your job to support her as this happens.
- *She doesn't expect you to "fix it."* Many partners feel frustrated because they feel inadequate or unable to fix the problem. She doesn't need you to try to take the problem away. This isn't like a leaky faucet that can be repaired with a new washer. Don't suggest quick-fix solutions. This isn't that kind of problem. She just needs you to listen.

- *Get the support you need so you can be there for her.* You need to take care of yourself by getting your own support from friends, family or professionals. You should make sure to get breaks from taking care of your family. Regular exercise or other stress-reducing activity is important, so you can remain the solid support for your wife. Provide a stand-in support person for her while you're gone.

- *Don't take it personally.* As the anxiety or irritability mounts in PPD sufferers, they tend to take it out on those closest to them, usually you. Don't allow yourself to become a verbal punching bag. It's not good for anyone concerned. She feels guilty after saying hurtful things to you. If you feel you didn't deserve to be snapped at, explain that to her calmly.

- *Just being there with and for her is doing a great deal.* Being present and letting her know you support her is often all she'll need. Ask her what words she needs to hear for reassurance, and say them to her often.

- *Lower your expectations.* Even a nondepressed postpartum woman cannot realistically be expected to cook dinner and clean house. She may be guilt-tripping herself about not measuring up to her own expectations and worrying that you will also be disappointed. Remind her that parenting your child and taking care of your home is also your job, not just hers. Your relationship and family will emerge from this crisis stronger than ever.

- *Let her sleep at night.* She needs five hours of uninterrupted sleep per night to complete a full sleep cycle and restore her biorhythms. If you want your wife back quicker, be on duty for half the night without disturbing her. Many dads have expressed how much closer they are to their children because of nighttime caretaking. If you can't be up with the baby during the night, hire someone who can take your place. A temporary baby nurse will be worth her weight in gold.

What to Say, What Not to Say

Say:
- "We will get through this."
- "I'm here for you."
- "I'm sorry you're suffering. That must feel awful."
- "I love you very much."
- "The baby loves you very much."
- "This is temporary. You'll get yourself back."
- "You're doing such a good job."
- "You're a great mom."
- "This isn't your fault. If I were ill, you wouldn't blame me."

Do not say:
- "Think about everything you have to feel happy about." She already knows everything she has to feel happy about. One of the reasons she feels so guilty is that she

is depressed despite these things.

- "Snap out of it." If she could, she would have already. She wouldn't wish this on anyone. A person cannot snap out of any illness.

From a Dad Who's Been There

This was written by Henry, Shoshana's husband, for Shoshana's newsletter, soon after her first depression had subsided:

You've just come home from a long day at work, hoping to find a happy home - and what you find makes you want to get back into the car and leave. Your wife is in tears, the baby is crying. The house is a mess, and forget about dinner. By now you know better than to ask how her day was. Her response is always the same. "I hate this 'mother' stuff. I don't want to be anyone's mother. I want my old life back. I want to be happy again." You shrug, go to hold the baby, and wonder why your wife is feeling this way, why she's not as happy as you are about the baby, and when she will snap out of it.

You're not alone. I lived with this scene every day for two years. Every ounce of my patience was tested, but I kept hoping that things would be "normal" again. I focused on my baby daughter, the one in the midst of this mess, and kept telling myself I'd be there for her.

Slowly, slowly, my wife recovered from the illness. Today, we have that happy home we both always wanted. Be patient and tolerant. Remember, it will get better.

FIVE

For Health Practitioners

The fact that you are reading this manual clearly indicates that you are a caring and concerned professional. Your guidance during this vulnerable and critical time will significantly impact the mental and physical well-being of women with perinatal mood disorders. It is important not to underreact or overreact to these women's symptoms. Just treat them as matter-of-factly as you would any other common perinatal experience, for example, gestational diabetes.

This chapter contains answers to the questions that we have been most frequently asked throughout the years regarding signs, symptoms, and treatment. Because a distressed woman's contact with a professional office includes the receptionist and nursing staff, it is imperative that the entire staff be knowledgeable about the information in this manual. We have created sections for primary care providers (family practitioners, internists, osteopaths, chiropractors), pediatricians, OB/GYN's and midwives, psychiatrists, birth doulas, postpartum doulas and visiting nurses, lactation consultants, childbirth educators, new parent group leaders, and adjunct professionals.

Please remember that warning signs of distress are not always obvious for a variety of reasons. Shame, guilt, or fear of judgment may cause the woman to hide her feelings. She may present more "socially acceptable" complaints, such as fatigue, headache, marital problems, or a fussy baby. Don't assume that just because a woman is smiling or well groomed, she is not suffering silently. We appreciate that you may be apprehensive about asking questions that could open a Pandora's box. She might feel accused of being a bad mom, and become defensive. But once she hears your matter-of-fact tone, and understands no shame is attached to postpartum illness, she will be able to accept the information. In the long run, you will be saving time and providing quality care.

Two postpartum depression screening inventories are available (see Resources). The Edinburgh Postnatal Depression Screening Scale was developed in 1987 in Britain. It is a 10 question self-report test. It has been translated into many languages and is used all over the world. It can be found on many Internet sites. More recently, Dr. Cheryl Beck developed the Postpartum Depression Screening Scale. It has been found to accurately screen for both postpartum depression and anxiety. Either of these screening inventories can easily be completed in a waiting room.

If you have assessed that a woman has a postpartum mood disorder, here are some basic "do's and don'ts."

What Not to Say

- *Join a new mom's group.* If a mother is clinically depressed or anxious, this may be a damaging suggestion, depending largely on the leader of the group. A depressed mother is already feeling different and inadequate compared to other new mothers. Attending a normal new mothers' group may intensify her alienation. If you know that the leader of the group is sensitive (such as those reading this manual) and discusses mood problems, this mom will be fine. Ideally, she should join a group specifically designed for mothers with postpartum depression and anxiety. Many of our clients belong to both types of groups: one to discuss the normal new mom stuff and the other to openly express more difficult feelings.

- *Take a vacation with your husband.* Although a change of scenery may be nice, the depressed mother takes her brain chemistry with her! Her anxiety and depression level may actually increase due to the financial investment, leaving her baby, and guilt that the trip did not "cure" her.

- *Exercise.* These mothers are feeling overwhelmed. Some have barely enough energy to wash a bottle, let alone go to the gym. Suggesting exercise to the chronically sleep-deprived mother can actually backfire and cause insomnia. Endorphins only work temporarily. Exercise will not cure her depression. When she's able to leave her house and take a short walk, she can be encouraged to do so. But, until then, this is just another setup for failure.

- *Do something nice for yourself.* This is always a good thing, but again, it will not be enough to regulate the depressed mother's neurotransmitters. This suggestion should be used only as part of a much larger treatment plan, not presented as a quick fix.

- *Sleep when the baby sleeps.* Even a nondepressed mother may have difficulty sleeping when the baby naps during the day. Especially for those mothers with high levels of anxiety, this will be an impossibility.

What is most important is that she sleeps *at night* when her baby sleeps.

What to Say

- These feelings are quite common.
- This is treatable.
- You will get well.
- Here is some information that will help you.

Primary Care Providers

As a primary care provider, you may have a longstanding relationship with your patient. You have a good sense of her mental and physical health history. This puts you in an advantageous position to evaluate her preconception risk, and provide appropriate direction. Your office may provide a safe haven should a pregnancy or postpartum mood problem arise. Please have information from the Resource section available, as well as local referrals.

PRECONCEPTION OR PRENATAL RISK ASSESSMENT

Questions to Ask

- Have you ever had depression, panic, extreme anxiety, bipolar disorder, psychosis, or eating disorder?
- Have you abused substances such as alcohol or drugs? Do you smoke?
- Are you taking any medications or herbs on a regular basis?
- Have you had a previous postpartum mood disorder?
- Have you ever taken any psychotropic medications?
- Have you ever had severe PMS or PMDD?
- Do you have any family history of mental illness or substance abuse?
- If pregnant, how have you been feeling physically and emotionally?
- Do you feel you have adequate emotional and physical support?
- Are you experiencing any major life stressors (for example, moving, job change, deaths, financial problems)?
- Have there been any health problems for you or the fetus?

POSTPARTUM RISK ASSESSMENT

Warning Signs
Any of the following can signal the development of a postpartum mood disorder:
- Missed appointments
- Excessive worrying (often about the mother's own health or health of baby)
- Looking unusually tired
- Requires support person to accompany to appointments
- Significant weight gain or loss
- Physical complaints with no apparent cause
- Breastfeeding problems

Questions to Ask
- Do you have any particular concerns?
- How are you sleeping (quality and quantity)?
- Have you had any unusual or scary thoughts?
- Are you getting physical and emotional help?
- Is your partner sharing the responsibilities of household and parenting?
- If nursing, how is the breastfeeding going? If using formula, when and how quickly did you wean? (Abrupt weaning can precipitate a mood disorder.)
- When was your last period? (First menses after delivery can be a precipitating factor.)
- How old is your child? If there are other children, what are their ages?
- Are you taking medications or herbs on a regular basis?

Pediatricians

The well-being of your patient is largely dependent on the well-being of the primary caregiver, usually the mother. It is well documented that the mental health of the mother has a tremendous impact on the emotional and physical development of the child. While the focus of the pediatric visit is primarily the baby, the health of the mother is a crucial component that must not be overlooked. In addition to the obvious milestones, the mother-baby relationship must be assessed. Have local referrals and information in the Resources section available.

Questions to ask the Mother

- How are *you* doing? (It is important to have good eye contact with the mother while you ask this question.)
- How are you feeling about motherhood?
- How are you sleeping (quality and quantity)?
- How is the baby sleeping? Who gets up at night with the baby?
- Can you sleep at night when everyone else is asleep? (Insomnia is a symptom of every mood disorder.)
- Do you generally feel like yourself?
- How is your appetite? What are you eating and drinking?
- Are you feeling moodier than normal (tearful, irritable, worried, or anxious)?
- If breastfeeding, how is it going? If formula-feeding, when and how quickly did you wean? (Abrupt weaning can precipitate a mood disorder.)
- Are you getting physical and emotional help?

- Is your partner sharing the responsibilities of household and parenting?
- Have there been any health problems for you or the baby?

POSTPARTUM RISK ASSESSMENT

Warning Signs in the Mother
- Evading questions about her own well-being
- Excessive worrying about the health of the baby despite reassurance (for instance, eating sufficiently, development, weight gain)
- Looking unusually tired
- Requires support person to accompany to appointments
- Dressing baby or herself too "perfectly" (happens often when she is overcompensating for feeling bad on the inside, or when manic)
- Excessive weight gain or loss
- Crying
- Discomfort with holding or responding to baby
- Feeling the baby doesn't like her

Warning Signs in the Baby
- Excessive weight gain or loss
- Delayed cognitive or language development
- Decreased responsiveness to mother
- Breastfeeding problems

OB/GYN Practitioners and Midwives

Your office has been a source of comfort and advice throughout the pregnancy. This intimate relationship makes it likely that a woman with postpartum distress will come to you for help if she feels depressed or anxious. However, many women will not be forthcoming with negative feelings or concerns unless specifically asked. Have local referrals and information in the Resources section available. Please monitor follow-up.

PRECONCEPTION OR PRENATAL RISK ASSESSMENT

Questions to Ask

- Have you ever had depression, panic, extreme anxiety, bipolar disorder, psychosis, or eating disorder?
- Have you abused substances such as alcohol or drugs? Do you smoke?
- Have you had a previous postpartum mood disorder?
- Have you ever taken any psychotropic medications?
- Have you ever had severe PMS or PMDD?
- Do you have any family history of mental illness or substance abuse?
- If pregnant, how have you been feeling physically and emotionally?
- Do you feel you have adequate emotional and physical support?
- Have you had a birth-related trauma (or other traumatic incident such as rape or sexual abuse)?
- Are you experiencing any particular life stressors (for example, moving, job change, deaths, or financial

problems)?

- Have there been any health problems for you or the fetus?
- Do you have a personal or family history of thyroid disorder?

POSTPARTUM RISK ASSESSMENT

Warning Signs
Any of the following can signal the development of a postpartum mood disorder:

- Missed appointments
- Excessive worrying (about the mother's own health or health of baby)
- Looking unusually tired
- Evading questions about her own well-being
- Requires support person to accompany to appointments
- Significant weight gain or loss
- Crying
- Physical complaints with no apparent cause
- Breastfeeding problems
- Flashback of previous trauma

Questions to Ask

- How are *you* doing? (Have good eye contact with the mother while you ask this question.)
- How are you feeling about motherhood?
- How are you sleeping (quality and quantity)?
- How is the baby sleeping? Who gets up at night with

the baby?

- Can you sleep at night when everyone else is asleep? (Insomnia is a symptom of every mood disorder.)
- Do you generally feel like yourself?
- How is your appetite? What are you eating and drinking? (A significant change in appetite either way is a warning sign.)
- Are you feeling moodier than normal (tearful, irritable, worried, or anxious)?
- If breastfeeding, how is it going? If formula-feeding, how quickly and when did you wean? (Abrupt weaning can precipitate a mood disorder.)
- When was your last period? (First menses after delivery can be a precipitating factor.)
- Are you getting adequate physical and emotional help?
- Is your partner sharing the responsibilities of household and parenting?
- Have there been any health problems for you or the baby?

Psychiatrists

Since you are the professionals who work most closely with psychotropic medications, many perinatal women will be referred to you for assessment and treatment of mood disorders. You play an integral role in this treatment team. Research findings and recommendations about medications in pregnancy and lactation are constantly changing. There have been some recent important findings in the area of medication management of perinatal mood disorders, which will be discussed later in this text. If you are only providing medication management, make sure you give your patients the name of a psychotherapist trained in perinatal mood disorders.

PRECONCEPTION OR PRENATAL RISK ASSESSMENT

Questions to Ask

- Have you ever had depression, panic, extreme anxiety, bipolar disorder, psychosis, or eating disorder?
- Have you abused substances such as alcohol or drugs? Do you smoke?
- Do you have a personal or family history of thyroid disorder?
- Have you had a previous postpartum mood disorder?
- Have you ever taken any psychotropic medications?
- Have you ever had severe PMS or PMDD?
- Do you have any family history of mental illness or substance abuse?
- If pregnant, how have you been feeling physically and emotionally?
- Do you feel you have adequate emotional and physical support?

- Are you experiencing any particular life stressors (for example, moving, job change, deaths, or financial problems)?
- Have there been any health problems for you or the fetus?

Warning Signs
Any of the following can signal the development of a postpartum mood disorder:

- Missed appointments
- Excessive worrying (about the mother's own health or health of baby)
- Looking unusually tired
- Requires support person to accompany to appointments
- Significant weight gain or loss
- Physical complaints with no apparent cause
- Breastfeeding problems

POSTPARTUM RISK ASSESSMENT

Questions to Ask

- How are *you* doing? (Have good eye contact with the mother while you ask this question.)
- How are you feeling about motherhood?
- How are you sleeping (quality and quantity)?
- How is the baby sleeping? Who gets up at night with the baby?
- Can you sleep at night when everyone else is asleep?
- Do you generally feel like yourself?
- How is your appetite? What are you eating and drinking?

- Are you feeling moodier than normal (tearful, irritable, worried, or anxious)?
- If breastfeeding, how is it going? If formula-feeding, when and how quickly did you wean? (Abrupt weaning can precipitate a mood disorder.)
- When was your last period? (First period after delivery can be a precipitating factor.)
- Are you getting adequate physical and emotional help?
- Is your partner sharing the responsibilities of household and parenting?
- How old is your baby? If there are other children, what are their ages?

Birth Doulas

Studies show that the use of a doula contributes to the reduction of postpartum depression. As a birth doula, you are in a unique position to observe early warning signs of emotional problems. Have local referrals and information in the Resources section available.

PRECONCEPTION OR PRENATAL RISK ASSESSMENT

Questions to Ask

- Have you ever had depression, panic, extreme anxiety, bipolar disorder, psychosis, or eating disorder?
- Have you abused substances such as alcohol or drugs? Do you smoke?
- Have you had a previous postpartum mood disorder?
- Have you ever taken any psychotropic medications?
- Have you ever had severe PMS or PMDD?
- Do you feel you have adequate emotional and physical support?
- Do you have any family history of mental illness or substance abuse?
- Have you had any previous birth-related trauma (or other traumatic incident such as rape or sexual abuse)?

Warning Signs

- Unwillingness to hold baby or allow others to care for the baby
- Excessive crying
- Expressing fear that baby doesn't like her
- Flashback, fear, or nightmares regarding previous trauma

Postpartum Doulas and Visiting Nurses

You have the opportunity to observe the home and social environments of the mother, which can give crucial information about her well-being and that of the family unit. Have local referrals and information in the Resources section available.

Questions to Ask
- Is there anything about your past that you think would be helpful for me to know (for example, depression, previous pregnancy or birth experience)?
- If nursing, how is it going?
- How are you sleeping?
- How is your appetite?
- Are you taking any medications or herbs on a regular basis?

Warning Signs in the Mother
- Unwillingness to hold baby
- Excessive crying
- Expressing fear that baby doesn't like her
- Unusual weight gain or loss
- Unusually clean or dirty house
- Lack of partner support, signs of marital conflict
- Excessive worry about herself or the baby
- Excessive concern about appearance of herself or baby
- Flashback, fear, or nightmares regarding previous trauma

Lactation Consultants

The role of a lactation consultant may superficially appear to be one-dimensional and relate only to the mechanics of breastfeeding. However, as we know, you are also providing tremendous emotional support. You may be the first professional to see the mother and baby during the initial postpartum weeks. Your intimate relationship with the mother at this vulnerable time allows you to observe and listen for potential emotional problems. Postpartum moms listen carefully to what you advise and are quite trusting of you. It is so important that you help each woman decide what is right for her. If her physical or emotional health is declining, it is obviously not good for the baby. You have a great deal of influence as to whether new mothers give themselves permission to take care of themselves (like five hours of uninterrupted sleep at night). Sometimes this will mean partial or complete weaning. Difficulty breastfeeding is associated with postpartum depression and anxiety. When a woman is weaning her baby, make sure she weans her own body very slowly even though her baby can wean "cold turkey." Abrupt weaning can precipitate a mood disorder especially when a woman is predisposed. If she is already suffering, abrupt weaning can greatly exacerbate her symptoms. Especially if a woman is depressed and not feeling good about herself, there can be a great amount of guilt if at any point she cannot or should not continue breastfeeding. What you say or do not say at that time can make a big difference regarding how she feels about herself as a mother. Have local referrals and information in the Resources section available, including an M.D. who has experience prescribing medication during lactation.

Warning Signs in the Mother
- Excessive crying
- Expressing fear that baby doesn't like her
- Excessive concern about baby despite reassurance (for example, questions about whether the baby is getting enough to eat)
- Rigidity about feeding schedules
- Unusual discomfort handling baby
- Inability to relax
- Poor milk production (could be caused by thyroid dysfunction)

Questions to Ask
- Do you have any concerns?
- How is your appetite?
- How are you feeling about being a mom?
- How are you feeling toward your baby?
- Are you able to sleep at night when the baby sleeps?

Childbirth Educators

So often we hear the lament, "Why didn't anyone warn us in our birthing classes about mood problems during and after pregnancy?" Even though your primary focus is on labor and delivery, you have a responsibility and opportunity to educate couples about perinatal mood disorders. This might be a difficult topic to discuss since no woman wants to think it could happen to her. If you know a professional who is an expert in this field, you can invite her or him to speak to your class. If not, bring the subject up in a matter-of-fact manner, the same way you would any other common pregnancy or postpartum experience. The rate of depression in pregnancy is 10 percent. Therefore, we can assume some of the women in your classes are already suffering and are at risk for a postpartum mood disorder. Your participants will not bring up this topic, so you need to. There is no danger in giving information, and there is great danger in omitting it. You have a captive audience with both members of the couple. The partner might be soaking up this information even if the mother-to-be is not. It is often the spouse who later recognizes the symptoms and encourages his wife to seek help. Hand out some information from the Resources section and the name and number of a professional trained in perinatal mood disorders. At the class reunion ask about participants' feelings about the challenges as well as the joys of parenthood. Be sure to call participants who did not attend the reunion. They may not be doing well and could be trying to avoid an uncomfortable situation.

New Parent Group Leaders

If there are ten women in your group, remember that, statistically, at least one of them will have postpartum depression. Rarely will this woman be brave enough to disclose her feelings, since she will most likely be experiencing guilt and shame. She will be aching for someone to open the door to this discussion and give her permission to express how she is really feeling. If spouses and fathers are present, ask them how they are doing. Encourage discussion about the normal feelings accompanying adjustment to parenting and the relationship to oneself, partner, baby, friends, and family. You can easily work in some facts about moods and behaviors that fall outside the realm of normal adjustment. For each new group, make sure this topic gets explored in a nonjudgmental manner. If you prefer, you can invite a professional with expertise in this area to lead a discussion. In any case, use the information in the Resources section and the names and numbers of local professionals trained in the area of postpartum disorders.

Adjunct Professionals

There are many other wonderful professionals who touch the lives of pregnant and postpartum women. For example, physical therapists and instructors in prenatal and postpartum exercise should mention the possibility of mood disorders, since you are encountering suffering women all the time. Above all, making the information in the Resources section available will support the pregnant and postpartum women with whom you work.

Treatment

Women seeking treatment often try to alleviate symptoms on their own before seeking the advice of a professional. This self-treatment may include potentially risky substances, such as alcohol or untested herbal or drug remedies. Little research has been done on the safety of herbs such as St. John's wort during pregnancy or nursing. Some herbal remedies and illegal drugs have been associated with serious harm to both mother and child, including birth defects, infant death, and liver toxicity. On the other hand, quite a bit of research has been conducted regarding the use of certain prescription medications during pregnancy and lactation that effectively combat perinatal mood disorders.

One important goal of treatment is to alleviate suffering as quickly as possible. While it is generally prudent to start medication at a low dosage, it should be increased as rapidly as possible to whatever the therapeutic dosage is for that woman. Under treating can lead to chronic symptomatology.

What follows here are guidelines only. All treatment must be individualized. For medication management we recommend the woman see a psychiatrist with expertise in treating perinatal mood disorders.

Treatment in Pregnancy

Pregnancy causes alterations in metabolism, therefore higher doses of medications may be required to reach therapeutic levels.

Antidepressants

Studies of selective serotonin reuptake inhibitors (SSRIs) or tricyclics (TCAs) used in pregnancy have revealed no increased risk for physical malformations, neonatal complications, miscarriage, or impairments in neurobehavioral development. At seven years of age exposed children tested normally on IQ and development tests. These data include first-trimester exposure. Based on current research, the preferred choices during pregnancy are Prozac and Zoloft, with Paxil and Celexa being second choices (less data). The top researchers maintain that there is no reason to change from one medication to another; go with what works and gets the quickest results.

Electroconvulsive Therapy (ECT)

ECT is considered an acceptable treatment for severe depression or psychosis in pregnancy. It may also be useful in treating bipolar disorder during pregnancy. ECT is not an appropriate treatment for prenatal anxiety, panic, or OCD.

Antipsychotics

Conventional high-potency antipsychotics, such as Haldol, are recommended over low-potency or atypical agents throughout pregnancy.

Mood Stabilizers

Recent research shows that the risk of Ebstein's (cardiac) anomaly with lithium use in the first trimester is under 1 percent. In one study no significant neurobehavioral or developmental problems were noted. A fetal cardiac ultrasound between weeks

18 and 20 is recommended for those with first trimester exposure. Lithium maintenance throughout pregnancy should be considered for women with severe bipolar disorders, since the risk of relapse is high. Reintroducing lithium after discontinuation in the first trimester does not protect well against relapse. Other mood stabilizers, such as Tegretol and Depakote, increase the rate of neural tube defects and are not recommended during pregnancy.

Antianxiety Medications

The literature regarding antianxiety exposure in utero for humans is limited and confusing. Few studies have been done on long term neurobehavioral outcomes. However, women with severe anxiety or panic disorder should be treated. Ativan is commonly used. The lowest effective dose for the shortest period of time is recommended.

Sleep Aids

If sleep is impaired due to depression or anxiety, medication may be necessary. TCAs such as Pamelor or Elavil may be useful at bedtime. Trazadone also has a sedative effect. Ativan and Ambien have faster rates of onset and, so far, are considered acceptable in pregnancy.

Treatment Postpartum

At least 10 percent of postpartum women suffer from postpartum thyroiditis. Sometimes this condition is temporary, but for others it can lead to chronic thyroiditis and hypothyroidism (Hashimoto's thyroiditis). Since thyroid disorders can cause depression and anxiety, thyroid dysfunction must be ruled out. The following tests are recommended for all women with postpartum mood complaints: free T4, TSH, anti-TPO, and anti-thyroglobulin.

Hormonal Therapies

Hormone therapy for postpartum depression is still being evaluated for efficacy. Research with estrogen holds promise for treatment of postpartum depression and postpartum psychosis. Women with postpartum depression or anxiety who choose oral contraceptives need to be monitored closely for mood changes, which are usually worse when a triphasic pill, as opposed to a monophasic pill, is used. Women with a history of increased moodiness on oral contraceptives should consider alternate methods of contraception. Synthetic progesterone (progestin) has been associated with a worsening of symptoms. Depo-Provera is not a good option, since it cannot be discontinued should it activate mood problems. Hormonal therapies are not currently recommended as sole treatment for postpartum psychiatric disorders.

Medications and Nursing

Antidepressants

Antidepressants of choice for lactating mothers are Zoloft, Paxil, Prozac, Celexa, and TCAs. The first choice for every woman should be a medication that has worked for her in the past or one that has been used successfully with a blood relative. The benefits of nursing far outweigh the theoretical risks of medications. The amounts of metabolites found in the infant's serum are so small they are almost impossible to detect. Behaviorally and developmentally these infants and children are normal.

Mood Stabilizers

Tegretol and Depakote are approved by the American Academy of Pediatrics (AAP) for breastfeeding mothers. Lithium is not recommended.

Antipsychotics

High-potency antipsychotics, such as Haldol, are used for nursing moms.

Sleep Aids

Ambien, Restoril, Trazadone, Pamelor, and Elavil are frequently prescribed for nursing moms.

Antianxiety Medication

Low doses of short acting medications such as Xanax or Ativan can be used on an occasional as-needed basis for anxiety, panic, and sleep.

Electroconvulsive Therapy (ECT)

ECT is considered an acceptable treatment for severe depression or psychosis postpartum, including for nursing mothers. It may also be useful in treating bipolar disorder postpartum. ECT is not an appropriate treatment for postpartum anxiety, panic, or OCD.

Medical Protocols

The chart below suggests treatments based upon the woman's history. Treatments should be followed in sequence, with Treatment 1 tried first, followed by Treatment 2 if necessary.

Although the treatment protocols that follow refer only to depression and psychosis, they are also effective in the treatment of OCD, anxiety and panic.

SSRI's are usually the first line medications in the treatment of OCD, anxiety and panic. For OCD, Luvox (fluvoxamine) and Anafranil (clomipramine) are second choices. Although Anafranil tends to have more side effects, it seems to be acceptable during pregnancy and lactation. Luvox has not been as well studied for use in pregnancy or lactation. It may be helpful to use low dose antianxiety medications on a short-term basis for anxiety and panic.

PRECONCEPTION		
History	**Treatment 1**	**Treatment 2**
One episode of major depression if on medication + asymptomatic for 6–12 months	Taper off medication + psychotherapy (monitor closely for relapse)	Resume medication + continue psychotherapy
Severe recurrent prior episodes	Continue medication + psychotherapy	
Mild major depression	Psychotherapy	Psychotherapy + medication
Severe major depression (first episode)	Medication + psychotherapy	
Bipolar disorder	Continue or switch to lithium + monitor closely by psychiatrist + psychotherapy	Switch to high potency antipsychotic if lithium-resistant or intolerant + continue psychotherapy

PREGNANCY (including first trimester)		
History	**Treatment 1**	**Treatment 2**
One episode mild major depression, currently in remission	Trial slow tapering medication + psychotherapy	Resume medication + psychotherapy
One episode severe major depression, currently in remission	Maintenance on medication + psychotherapy	
Mild major depression, first or recurrent	Psychotherapy	Medication + psychotherapy*
Severe major depression, first episode	Medication + psychotherapy	ECT + psychotherapy
Recurrence or relapse of depression if off medication if mild major depression	Psychotherapy	Resume medication + psychotherapy
Severe major depression, currently symptomatic	Resume medication + psychotherapy	ECT + psychotherapy
Psychosis in any trimester (Note: do not rely on psychosocial interventions alone; requires hospitalization)	Antipsychotic + psychotherapy Add mood stabilizer or antidepressant if needed once stable Or ECT + psychotherapy	

If this is not successful, further treatment of ECT + psychotherapy should be considered.

POSTPARTUM		
History	**Treatment 1**	**Treatment 2**
Mild major depression	Psychotherapy	Psychotherapy + medication
Severe major depression	Psychotherapy + medication	Consider ECT
Postpartum psychosis (Note: hospitalization required. Do not rely on psychosocial interventions alone.)	Antipsychotic + psychotherapy Add mood stabilizer or antidepressant if needed once stable Or ECT + psychotherapy	

PREVENTION OF POSTPARTUM DEPRESSION IN WOMEN WITH HISTORY OF DEPRESSION, ANXIETY, OTHER MOOD DISORDER, OR PRIOR PPD		
History	**Treatment 1**	**Treatment 2**
First pregnancy	Meet with psychotherapist when risk identified (preconception or pregnancy) + psychoeducation for woman and partner	Intervention (refer to pregnancy treatment protocol) if symptomatic
Prior postpartum depression	Psychoeducation for woman and partner as early as possible + start antidepressant 2–4 weeks before delivery + psychotherapy Or start anti-depressant immediately after delivery + psychotherapy	
Prior postpartum psychosis	Start lithium upon delivery + psychotherapy	

Resources

Organizations

Postpartum Support International
(805) 967-7636
www.postpartum.net
Telephone support and international directory of members.
Annual conference.

The Marcé Society
PO Box 30853
London, England W12OXG
www.marcesociety.com
International organization dedicated to scientific research in the field.
Annual conference.

North American Society for Psychosocial OB/GYN
409 12th Street, S.W.
Washington, DC 20024-2188
(202) 863-1628
www.naspog.com
Annual conference.

Depression After Delivery
(800) 944-4PPD
www.depressionafterdelivery.com
Answering machine. Will send packet on PPD with some resources.

Postpartum Health Alliance (California's state organization)
20052 Jessee Ct.
Castro Valley, CA 94552
(510) 889-6017
www.postpartumhealthalliance.org
Annual training.

Books

Dunnewold, Ann. *Evaluation and Treatment of Postpartum Emotional Disorders.* Sarasota, Florida: Professional Resource Press, 1997.

Dunnewold, Ann, and Diane Sanford. *Postpartum Survival Guide.* Oakland, California: New Harbinger Press, 1994.

Kendall-Tackett, Kathleen, and Glenda Kantor. *Postpartum Depression: A Comprehensive Approach for Nurses.* Newbury Park, California: Sage Publications, 1993.

Kleiman, Karen. *The Postpartum Husband.* Philadelphia: Xlibris, 2000.

Kleiman, Karen, and Valerie Raskin. *This Isn't What I Expected.* New York: Bantam Books, 1994.

Miller, Laura, ed. *Postpartum Mood Disorders.* Washington, D.C.: American Psychiatric Press, 1999.

Misri, Shaila. *Shouldn't I Be Happy?: Emotional Problems of Pregnant and Postpartum Women.* New York: Free Press, 1995.

Raskin, Valerie. *When Words Are Not Enough: The Women's Prescription for Depression and Anxiety.* New York: Broadway Books, 1997.

Roan, Sharon. *Postpartum Depression: Every Woman's Guide to Diagnosis, Treatment, and Prevention.* Hollbrook, Massachusetts: Adams Media Corporation, 1997.

Robin, Peggy. *Bottlefeeding Without Guilt: A Reassuring Guide for Loving Parents.* Roseville, California: Prima Publishing, 1996.

Sebastian, Linda. *Overcoming Postpartum Depression and Anxiety.* Omaha: Addicus Books, 1998.

Sichel, Deborah, and Jeanne Driscoll. *Women's Moods.* New York: William Morrow and Co., 1999.

Steiner, Meir, and Kim Yonkers. *Depression in Women: Mood Disorders Associated with Reproductive Cyclicity.* Pfizer, Inc., 1998.

Treatment of Depression in Women 2001, Postgraduate Medicine: A Special Report. The Expert Consensus Guideline Series. White Plains, NY: Expert Knowledge Systems. Can be ordered from the publisher at 21 Bloomingdale Rd., White Plains, NY, 10605 for $12.95.

Journal Articles

Prenatal Screening

Beck, C. A checklist to identify women at risk for developing postpartum depression. *J Obstet Gynecol Neonatal Nurs.* Jan.-Feb. 1998;27(1):39-46

Posner, N., et al. Screening for postpartum depression; an antepartum questionnaire. *J Reprod Med.* 1997;42:207-215

Postpartum Screening

Cox, J.L., et. al. Detection of postnatal depression: development of the 10-item Edinburgh Postnatal Depression Scale. *British Journal of Psychiatry 1987*; 150:782-786.

Postpartum Depression Screening Scale (PDSS). By Cheryl Tatano Beck, D.N.Sc., and Robert Gable, Ed.D. Available through Western Psychological Services (800) 648-8857

Postpartum Depression

Hendrick, V., et al. Postpartum and nonpostpartum depression: differences in presentation and response to pharmacologic treatment. *Depression and Anxiety.* 2000;11:66-72

Nonacs, R., and Cohen, L.S. Postpartum mood disorders: diagnosis and treatment guidelines. *J Clin Psychiatry.* 1998;59 (suppl 2):34-40.

Stowe, Z.N. and Nemeroff, C.B. Women At Risk For Postpartum–Onset Major Depression. *Am J. Obstet.* Gynecol. August 1995; 173(2):639-644

Medications During Pregnancy

Altshuler, L., et al. Pharmacologic management of psychiatric illness during pregnancy: dilemmas and guidelines. *Am J Psychiatry.* May 1996;153:592-606.

Barki, J., Kravitz, H., Berki, T. Psychotropic medications in pregnancy. *Psychiatric Annals.* Sept. 1998;28:486-497.

Cohen, L. Pharmacologic treatment of depression in women: PMS, pregnancy, and the postpartum period. *Depression and Anxiety.* 1998;8, suppl 1:18-26.

Kulin, N., et al. Pregnancy outcome following maternal use of the new selective serotonin reuptake inhibitors. *JAMA.* 1998;279(8):609-610.

Nulman, I., et al. Neurodevelopment of children exposed in utero to antidepressant drugs. *NEJM.* 1997;336 (4):258-62.

Wisner, K.L. et al, Pharmacologic treatment of depression during pregnancy. *JAMA* 1999;282:1264-1269.

Medications and Lactation

Birnbaum, C. S., et al. Serum concentrations of antidepressants and benzodiazepines in nursing infants: a case series. *Pediatrics.* 1999;104:11

Burt, V. K., et al. The use of psychotropic medications during breastfeeding. *Am J Psychiatry.* 2001;158:1001-1009.

Chaudron, L. When and how to use mood stabilizers during breastfeeding. *Primary Care Update* OB/GYNs, 2000;7(3)

Chaudron, L., and Jefferson, W. Mood stabilizers during breastfeeding: a review. *J Clin Psychiatry.* 2000; 61:79-90.

Llewellyn, A., and Stowe, Z.. Psychotropic medications in lactation. *J Clin Psychiatry.* 1998;59(suppl 2):41-52.

Stowe, Z., et al. Paroxetine in human breast milk and nursing infants. *Am J Psychiatry.* 2000;157:185-189.

Suri, R. A., et al. Managing psychiatric medications in the breastfeeding woman. *Medscape Women's Health.* 1998; 3(1)

Wisner K.L., et al. Antidepressant treatment during breastfeeding. *Am J Psychiatry.* 1996;153(9):1132-1137.

QUICK ORDER FORM

Beyond the Blues
Prenatal & Postpartum Depression

INTERNET: www.beyondtheblues.com
Credit cards accepted over the Internet

POSTAL ORDER: (check or money order):
Moodswings Press, 1050 Windsor St., San Jose, CA 95129-2837

Name: _____

Address: _____

City: _____ State: _____ Zip: _____

Quantity: _____ @ $19.95 per book $_____
Please add $5.00 shipping per book $_____
California residents please add 7.25% ($1.45)
Santa Clara County residents add 8.25% ($1.65)

    Sales Tax $_____

Total Enclosed $_____

PLEASE ALLOW 7-10 BUSINESS DAYS FOR DELIVERY

CONTACT US FOR BULK DISCOUNT RATES